Twenty to Make
Modern Friendship Bracelets

Pam Leach

Search Press

OCT 2 4 2014

First published in Great Britain 2014

Search Press Limited
Wellwood, North Farm Road,
Tunbridge Wells, Kent TN2 3DR

Text copyright © Pam Leach 2014

Illustrations on pages 6 and 7 by Bess Harding
Photographs by Paul Bricknell (cover and pages 5,
17, 22, 29, 33, 38, 40, 44, 46 and 48); all other
photographs by Angela Spain

Photographs and design copyright
© Search Press Ltd 2014

Print ISBN: 978-1-78221-016-0
Epub ISBN: 978-1-78126-211-5
Mobi ISBN: 978-1-78126-212-2

The Publishers and author can accept no
responsibility for any consequences arising from
the information, advice or instructions given in
this publication.

Suppliers

Although the components used in the designs are widely available,
they can all be obtained from the Beads Direct website:
www.beadsdirect.co.uk.
For details, see the author's note on page 48.

Printed in China

Contributors

It is practically impossible to be part of the
Beads Direct team and not be inspired to
make jewellery – I am fortunate to work with
some very talented people!

I would particularly like to thank those who
have contributed their designs to this book –
Laura Bajor, Vicki Downes,
Claire Humpherson, Stacy Hunt and
Sandy Yeates – 'thank you' to you all.

On behalf of Beads Direct, I would also
like to thank Search Press for inviting us to
produce this book for you.

Contents

Introduction

Traditionally, friendship bracelets were created by North American Indians using a simple piece of knotted cord, but more recently they have evolved to include a multitude of materials, techniques and styles. Designs now use leather and suede or ribbon and cord and feature charms and crystals – there are no rules and you are limited only by your imagination! However, the spirit of the friendship bracelet remains – they are given as a gift to celebrate and confirm a special friendship.

The designs in this book range from those that are beautifully simple and easy to make, to some that may take a little longer but are well worth the effort! Some of the designs use simple knotting techniques, and once you have mastered these techniques there are no limits to the designs that you can make.

There is nothing better than wearing a bracelet or giving one as a gift that you have taken the care to create yourself. With just the addition of a charm or the choice of the colour of your cord, your design becomes unique.

We hope that you will be inspired to try some of the designs in this book, and then to go on to create your own personalised friendship bracelets to share with your family and friends.

Pam Leach and the Beads Direct team.

Square knots

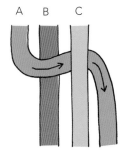

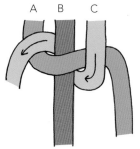

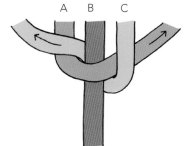

1 Pass cord A over B and under C.

2 Pass cord C under B and over A.

3 Pull cord A and cord C tight to create half the square knot.

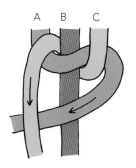

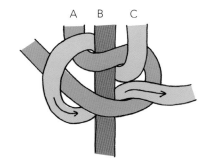

4 Pass cord A over B and under C.

5 Pass cord C over A, under B and over A. Pull the cords tight to complete the square knot.

Four-strand plait (braid)

1 Tie four cords together with a knot at one end. Lay them flat and secure them to the surface using either a pin or a heavy weight. Separate the strands.

2 Keeping the tension tight throughout, pass the far right-hand cord (D) under the middle two cords (B and C).

3 Pass the same cord (D) over the cord to its right (B).

4 Now pass the far left-hand cord (A) under the middle two cords, which are now B and D.

5 Pass the same cord (A) over the cord to its left (D).

6 Repeat steps 2 to 5 until the four-strand plait (braid) is complete. Remember to keep the tension tight all the time.

Love Heart Ceramics

Materials:

Designer: Pam Leach

1m (40in) of pink 1.5mm waxed nylon cord

I x ceramic heart

2 x metal heart beads

2 x round metal beads

Tools:

Scissors

Thread zapper or clear contact glue

Instructions:

1 Cut two pieces of waxed nylon cord each 30cm (12in) in length.

2 Thread both strands through the holes in the ceramic heart and position the heart in the centre on the lengths of the two strands.

3 On one strand of the cord, tie a simple knot approximately 4cm (1½in) either side of the ceramic heart. Thread on a metal heart bead to each side and tie another knot to hold in place.

4 Cross both double threads over to form a complete circle and with the remaining 40cm (16in) of cord, tie eight square knots (see page 6) over all four threads to create a sliding knot. Use either a thread zapper to bond the ends of the cord or use clear glue. Trim any excess.

5 Thread a round metal bead on to the two remaining long threads and knot to secure.

Flower Power Ceramics

The brighter version shown opposite is made in exactly the same way using vibrant orange and greens, a flower-shaped ceramic bead and metal star beads.

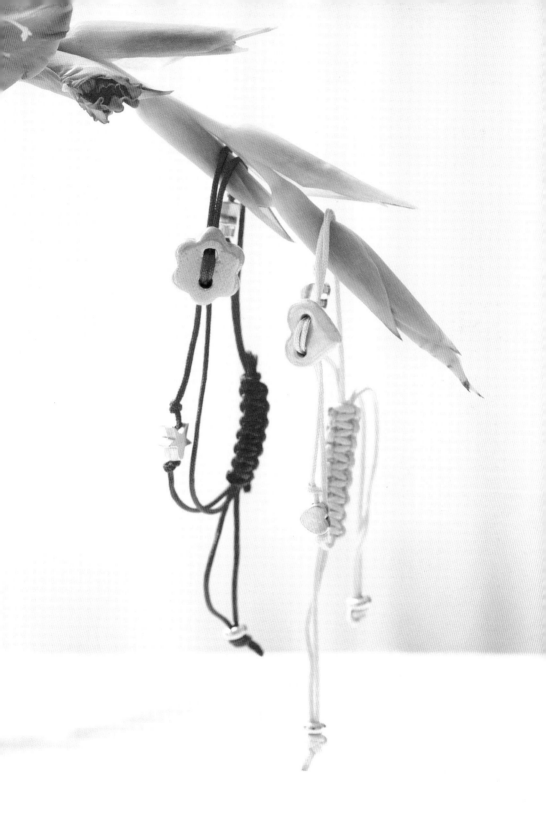

Braided Flower Bracelet

Materials:

Designer: Laura Bajor

1 x hand-painted Zamak flower bead
1m (40in) of orange 1mm waxed cotton cord
1m (40in) of green 1mm waxed cotton cord

Tools:

Scissors

Instructions:

1 Take the two pieces of waxed cotton cord, fold them in half from the centre and tie a knot to create a loop. This loop needs to be big enough to fit the flower charm through.

2 Gather all four cords and start your four-strand plait (braid) (see instructions on page 7).

3 Once you are happy with the size of your bracelet, attach the flower bead to the end of the cords and secure with a knot.

A Touch of Romance

Try pink and blue cords and a coordinating flower bead to create a more romantic effect.

Free Spirit

Materials:

Designer: Claire Humpherson

1 x Zamak bracelet half bar

17 x gold-coloured hand-crafted brass beads

15 x blue hand-crafted brass beads

4 x silver star charm beads

75cm (30in) of metallic blue 3mm round leather cord

75cm (30in) of metallic blue 2mm round leather cord

2 x blue Shamballa fashion rondelle beads

1 x gold-coloured Shamballa fashion rondelle bead

Tools:

Scissors

Clear contact glue

Instructions:

1 Double each length of cord over. Thread a Shamballa fashion rondelle bead over the two strands of the 3mm cord and push towards the folded end to create a loop. Do the same with the 2mm cord using one of the brass beads.

2 Thread the remaining beads randomly on to the four strands. With the 2mm cord, alternate between threading several beads on to each strand separately and threading them through both cords together.

3 Check that the leather wraps around your wrist twice and cut off any excess. Trim the leather diagonally to make it easier to place into the bracelet bar.

4 Glue all four ends of the leather cords into the bracelet bar. Once dry, wrap around twice and hook the loops over the bar to fasten.

Boho Bracelet

A simple change of colour, and a whole new look can be created!

Infinity

Materials:

Designer: Sandy Yeates

2m (80in) of orange and red flat
    parachute cord

1 x Zamak orange infinity connector charm

1 x spring toggle lock clasp

Tools:

Scissors

Thread zapper or clear contact glue

Instructions:

1 Cut two lengths of cord, one 40cm (16in) and
one 150cm (60in).

2 Take the longer cord and start square knotting
(see page 6) approximately 10cm (4in) from one
end of the 40cm cord. Complete six square knots.

3 Place the infinity connector charm on to the centre cord
and thread the cord through the charm from front to back.

4 Flip the bracelet over and square knot at the back of the
infinity charm. Complete two square knots.

5 Thread the centre cord back through to the front of the charm
and make a further six square knots.

6 Take the two cord ends from the 40cm (16in) cord and thread
in opposite directions through the spring toggle lock clasp. Tie a
knot at the end of each cord.

7 Trim all the ends and either seal with the thread zapper or
secure with clear glue.

Monochrome
*Create a black and white
paracord bracelet for a
stylish alternative.*

Rose Quartz Plait

Materials:

2.4m (96in) of six-strand floss thread

20 x rose quartz semi-precious chips, approximately 5 x 8mm

36 x rose gold 3mm round beads

Tools:

Scissors

Designer: Laura Bajor

Instructions:

1 Cut three pieces of thread, each approximately 80cm (32in) in length.

2 Put the three pieces together and form a loop at one end. Secure with a simple double knot. The loop should be just large enough to fit over two of the rose quartz chips comfortably. Keep these two chips to one side.

3 Separate out the three strands.

4 On one strand, thread on the beads in the following pattern: two 3mm round beads, one rose quartz chip.

5 On the second strand, thread one 3mm round bead and then one rose quartz chip, then thread the remaining beads on in the pattern: two 3mm round beads, one rose quartz chip.

6 Leave the third strand without any beads.

7 Now start plaiting (braiding) the three strands, manipulating the beads in place between each wrap.

8 When your bracelet is the desired length, continue plaiting without any beads for approximately 2cm (¾in) and then thread on to two of the strands the two rose quartz chips that were set aside earlier.

9 Tie an overhand knot to secure these beads in place.

10 Trim off all the excess ends.

Multi Gemstone Plait
Using a mix of gemstone chips creates a natural feel for this plaited (braided) bracelet.

Love Charm Bracelet

Materials:

Designer: Laura Bajor

60cm (24in) of red 2mm round leather cord

8 x gold-coloured charms of your choice; I've chosen 2 heart charms, an anchor charm, a red parcel charm, a hand charm and a red crystal charm

8 x gold-coloured jump rings

2 x 6mm gold-coloured cord ends

1 x gold-coloured toggle clasp

Tools:

Scissors

Snipe nose pliers

Flat nose pliers

Clear contact glue

Instructions:

1 Cut three 20cm (8in) pieces of the leather cord.

2 Using the pliers, attach jump rings to your charms. Use the remaining two jump rings to join each part of the toggle clasp to a cord end.

3 Thread two charms on to each piece of leather cord.

4 Make a knot to the right of each charm. Position the knots so that all the charms are spaced evenly and can be seen clearly. You could add in more charms if you wish.

5 Glue the very ends of the cords together, then put some glue into each cord end and glue in the ends of the leather.

6 Allow the glue to dry.

My Favourite Things

Use silver charms and black leather to create a more understated effect.

Pretty in Pink

Designer: Pam Leach

Materials:

50cm (20in) of pink 1mm waxed cotton cord

1m (40in) of Liberty print spaghetti ribbon

5 x silver charms of your choice; I've chosen an owl charm, a bird charm, a dragonfly charm, a butterfly charm and a flying bird charm

1 x silver heart button

2 x titanium-plated 7mm clam shell ribbon ends

2 x 4mm silver-plated round beads

5 x 6mm jump rings

Tools:

Scissors

Flat nose pliers

Snipe nose pliers

Instructions:

1 Fold the 50cm (20in) length of waxed cotton cord in half and tie a knot 2cm (¾in) from the folded end to form a loop. The loop needs to be large enough to go over the heart button.

2 Fold the ribbon in half and tie it over the knot forming the loop. Commence square knotting (see page 6) over the two strands of waxed cotton cord. Continue until you have used all of the ribbon.

3 Use your pliers to clamp one clam shell ribbon end over the raw ends of the ribbon. Clamp the other clam shell end over the knot at the start of the square knotting.

4 Using your pliers, attach jump rings to the charms. Attach two of the charms to the clam shells and loop the other three charms through the ribbon.

5 Thread the heart button on to the loose ends of the waxed cotton and secure with a knot approximately 5cm (2in) from the end. Thread a 4mm silver-plated round bead on to each end and finish with a knot.

Feeling Blue

Try using dark blue fabric and rose gold charms to create a more sophisticated feel to this pretty bracelet.

Head in the Clouds

Designer: Laura Bajor

Materials:

3.5m (140in) of light blue 0.5mm satin cord

1 x cloud connector charm

4 x 2mm silver-plated round beads

Tools:

Scissors

Clear contact glue

Instructions:

1 Cut two pieces of satin cord each 40cm (16in) long.

2 Thread one piece through each loop at either end of the cloud connector charm. Pull each cord through to create two equal strands.

3 Cut a piece of satin cord 1m (40in) long and create 6cm (2¼in) of square knotting (see page 6) starting at the cloud connector charm. Cut a second piece of satin cord 1m (40in) long and repeat on the other side of the charm. Cross the two remaining ends of the cord.

4 Cut a 50cm (20in) piece of satin cord. Use it to create square knots over the two ends of the 40cm (16in) cord, forming a sliding knot. The number of square knots you need will depend on the size of the bracelet.

5 Thread two silver-plated round beads on to each loose end and tie knots to secure.

6 Trim all the ends and secure with a dab of clear contact glue.

Mini Love Braids

You can change the sentiment of these mini braided bracelets by using different colours and different connector charms.

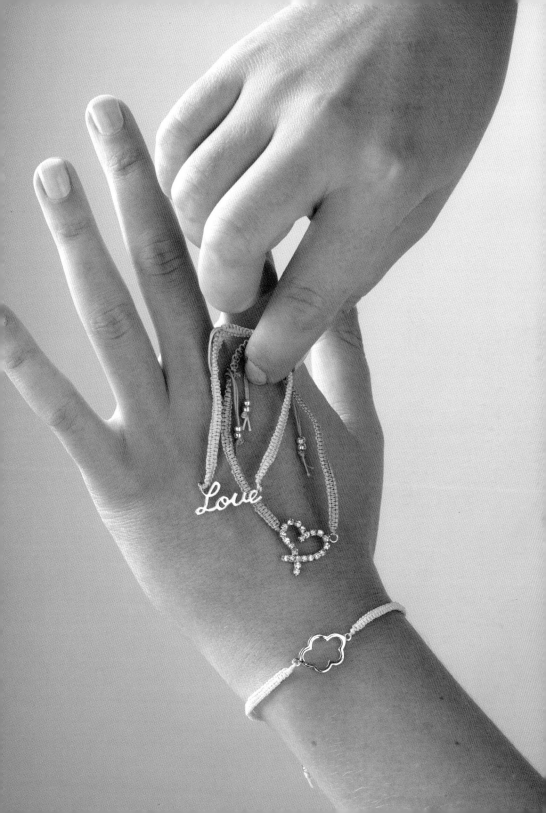

Valentine's Gift

Materials:

Designer: Pam Leach

30cm (12in) of black 1mm waxed nylon cord

3m (120in) of black 1.5mm waxed nylon cord

1 x 4mm silver-plated charm carrier

1 x silver-plated parcel charm with ruby crystal

1 x 5mm silver-plated jump ring

4 x Crystal clear silver-plated 8mm rondelles

2 x 4mm silver-plated round beads

Tools:

Scissors

Snipe nose pliers

Flat nose pliers

Thread zapper or clear
    contact glue

Instructions:

1 Attach the charm to the charm carrier with the jump ring, using the pliers to open and close the ring. Thread the charm carrier on to the 30cm (12in) length of 1mm waxed nylon cord and position it in the centre.

2 Cut 30cm (12in) of 1.5mm waxed nylon cord and complete five square knots (see page 6) to one side of the charm carrier. Trim the ends and secure. Thread on one rondelle and complete a further five square knots with another 30cm (12in) length of waxed nylon cord. Trim the ends and secure. Thread on another rondelle and complete a further six square knots with another 30cm (12in) length of 1.5mm waxed cotton cord. Trim the ends and secure.

3 Repeat step 2 on the other side of the charm carrier.

4 Cross over the loose ends of the 1mm waxed nylon cord and complete eight square knots over both strands using 40cm (16in) of 1.5mm waxed nylon cord to create a sliding knot.

5 Add one 4mm silver-plated round bead to each end of the 1mm cord and secure with a simple knot. Trim all the ends and seal using either a thread zapper or clear glue.

Gift-Wrapped Amethyst
The gold and amethyst version uses the same techniques but has a very different look.

Crystal Bangle

Materials:

1 x rose-gold plated bangle base

1.5m (60in) of dark pink 0.5mm waxed cotton cord

20 x 4mm crystal bicones in crystal rose gold

2 x 4mm gold-plated jump rings

Tools:

Scissors

Flat nose pliers

Snipe nose pliers

Clear contact glue

Designer: Pam Leach

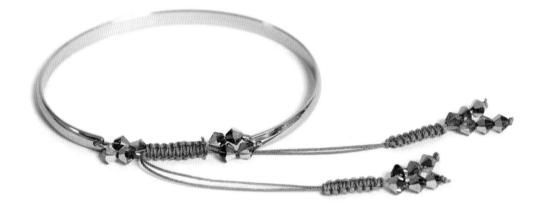

Instructions:

1 Connect a jump ring to each end of the bangle, using the pliers to open and close the ring.

2 Cut two 30cm (12in) lengths of waxed cotton cord and thread one strand through each jump ring. Loop the cord in half and thread two bicone beads on to each end of the thread. Position the bicone beads at the top of the thread near the bangle. Repeat for both sides of the bangle.

3 Cross the four strands of thread and, using a new piece of length 30cm (12in), create eight square knots (see page 6) over all four strands to form a sliding knot. Trim and secure the ends with a dab of clear glue.

4 Thread three bicone beads on to each of the four strands of cord and secure each end with a simple knot.

5 Cut a 30cm (12in) length of cord and create eight square knots above the bicone beads on one side of the bracelet. Trim the ends and secure.

6 Repeat step 5 on the other side of the bracelet.

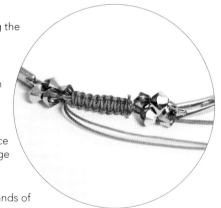

Silver Style

Stylish silver is used for an understated alternative design.

Summer Butterflies

Materials:

50cm (20in) of black 1mm
  waxed nylon cord

8 x ceramic butterfly beads in
  red, green, purple and blue

Tools:

Scissors

Thread zapper or
  clear contact glue

Designer: Laura Bajor

Instructions:

1 Cut a length of cord 35cm (14in) long and tie a knot
8cm (3¼in) from one end.

2 Thread your first bead on to the cord from the long
end and slide it up to the knot. Tie a knot after the
bead to hold it in place.

3 Continue to thread on your beads and knot after
each one until all the beads are used.

4 Cross the two cord ends and, using the remaining
piece of cord, complete five square knots (see page 6)
over the two strands to form a sliding knot.

5 Tie a simple knot in each of the cord ends.

6 Trim all the ends and finish using either the thread zapper or
clear glue.

Tip

*If you are using beads with a
slightly larger hole, use a double
strand of cord to create a larger
knot between the beads.*

Hearts and Butterflies
Use fuchsia pink butterfly beads, coin beads and heart beads alternating with 10mm silver beads to create a feminine look for summer.

Moonlight Reflections

Materials:

Designer: Vicki Downes

1 x titanium-plated connector holder
1 x 12mm flat-back foiled crystal
60cm (24in) of blue 2mm elasticated shock cord
5 x antique silver Zamak oval rings
4 x titanium-plated 7mm spacer beads

Purple Days

*You can achieve different looks
by changing the colours used
and being creative with the
oval rings.*

Tools:

Scissors
G-S Hypo cement

Instructions:

1 Cut two pieces of elastic cord approximately 30cm (12in) long.
Thread one through each side of the connector holder so that both
strands are the same length.

2 Thread an oval ring on to each side and knot the strands to hold
them in place next to the connector holder.

3 Thread another oval ring on to each pair of cords. Now thread all
four ends through one oval ring.

4 Thread a titanium-plated spacer bead on to the end of each cord
and then tie a knot. Cut off any excess elastic.

5 Glue the large crystal into the connector holder and leave to dry.

Rose Gold Pearl Wrap

Materials:

60cm (24in) of pearl 1mm round leather cord

1 x crystal rose gold 10mm button

2m (80in) of white Nymo beading thread

66 x 4mm glass pearls in rose gold

Tools:

Designer: Laura Bajor

Scissors

Beading needle

Instructions:

1 Thread the button on to the leather cord so that it sits in the middle. Fold the leather and tie an overhand knot under the button. You should have two strands of leather that are equal in length.

2 Thread the Nymo thread into your beading needle. Attach the Nymo thread on to the leather cord under the button so that it is hidden.

3 Bring your thread through below the knot and place it between the two strands of leather.

4 Wrap the thread over and under the right-hand strand, then over and under the left-hand strand. It should now be back in the centre, between the two leather strands. This sequence is also used when adding the beads.

5 Repeat step 4 two or three times, then thread on one bead, wrap the thread over and under the right-hand strand, take the thread back through the bead, and wrap the thread over and under the left-hand strand.

6 Add two beads. Wrap the thread over and under the right-hand strand, take the thread back through the two beads, then wrap it over and under the left-hand strand.

7 Repeat step 6 until your bracelet is the desired length. Finish by adding just one bead and wrap the thread over and under the right-hand strand followed by the left-hand strand.

8 Do two or three more wraps, then tie the leather strands and the thread together where the beads end using an overhand knot.

9 Leave a gap big enough for the button to fit through, then tie an overhand knot. Leave the same size gap again and then tie another overhand knot. Trim away any excess leather. Use one of the two gaps to secure the bracelet on your wrist. The two gaps allow the bracelet to be adjusted to a different size.

Little Red Devil

Black leather strands and red beads create a glamorous alternative to this pretty design.

Whirlpool Magic

Materials:

Designer: Sandy Yeates

90cm (36in) of black 2mm round leather cord

50cm (20in) of silver-plated ball chain

1m (40in) of orange 1mm waxed cotton cord

1 x Clown Fish beach bead

Tools:

Scissors

Instructions:

1 Fold the black leather cord in half to form a loop. The loop will need to be big enough to fit around the beach bead, which will act as the clasp. Wrap the end of the waxed cotton cord around the base of the loop at least 3 to 6 times, working downwards (away from the loop). This secures the waxed cord and will be the start of the bracelet.

2 Place the ball chain along the leather cord with the end of the chain level with the end of the wrap. Holding the ball chain against the leather cord, wrap the waxed cord around the leather tightly between each ball. Continue wrapping until your bracelet is the required length

3 When you have reached the end of the ball chain, wrap the cotton cord around the leather strands two or three more times. Tie a knot with all three strands.

4 Thread the beach bead through the strands and tie a knot to secure. Trim the cords with scissors.

Beach Babe

Using turquoise as your main colour and replacing the Clown Fish beach bead with a Sea Breeze Beach bead creates a completely different look.

Festival Fun

Materials:

Designer: Laura Bajor

2 x large flat cord ends, 7 x 25mm (¼ x 1in)

5 x 6mm silver jump rings

1 x 10mm lobster clasp

2 x 12cm (5in) lengths of 20mm Liberty print cotton ribbon

1 x 12cm (5in) length of flat plaited (braided) white cord

1 x 12cm (5in) length of 4mm silver-plated cup chain

18 x 6mm dark blue pearls

30cm (12in) of 0.5mm waxed cotton cord

30cm (12in) of 2.5mm red suede cord

Tools:

Scissors

Flat nose pliers

Snipe nose pliers

Clear contact glue

Instructions:

1 Thread the pearls on to the 0.5mm waxed cotton cord, knotting in between each pearl. Leave 4cm (1½in) of cord at each end.

2 Fold the red suede cord in half and knot it around the cup chain, weaving it around the crystals to create a wrapped effect. Secure the suede cord to each end of the cup chain with a small dab of glue. Trim the ends of the suede.

3 Now take the two lengths of ribbon and fold and press them in half lengthways.

4 Gather together the two fabric ribbons, the flat plaited (braided) cord, the cup chain and the strand of pearls, and arrange them in your preferred order. Align the ends and insert them into one of the cord ends. Secure them using glue. Allow to dry.

5 Take the other ends of all the strands and secure them into the other cord end – you may need to adjust the lengths of the strands depending on your wrist size. Remember you still have to attach the jump rings and lobster clasp so allow for these too.

6 Using pliers to open and close the jump rings, attach three jump rings to one cord end and two jump rings and the lobster clasp to the other end. You can adjust the size of your bracelet by using either more or less jump rings.

Random Strands

Vary the colours, and use any left-over cords, ribbons and beads to make this pretty bracelet.

Candy Sugar Bracelet

Materials:

11 x Pandora-style wood beads in various colours, 14 x 8mm (½ x ¼in)

1.7m (68in) of blue 2mm round leather cord

Tools:

Scissors

Designer: Laura Bajor

Instructions:

1 Cut two pieces of leather cord, one approximately 70cm (28in) the other 100cm (40in) long.

2 Take the smaller piece and fold it in half. Pin the fold to a surface. This is your base strand.

3 Tie the longer piece to the base piece just below the fold, leaving a large enough loop to fit over one wood bead. Ensure the two strands of the longer piece are even in length and lie either side of the base strand.

4 Wrap the right-hand strand around the base strand, going over the base strand and then back under. Do the same with the left-hand strand.

5 Now thread a bead on to the right-hand strand, and then thread the left-hand strand through the same bead. The threads will have swapped sides. Pull the strands tight.

6 Wrap the outer strands around the base strand, as you did in step 4.

7 Repeat steps 5 and 6 until you've added all the beads except one.

8 Knot the two longer strands together, then thread all four strands through your remaining wood bead. Knot all the four strands together. Trim any excess threads.

9 To secure the bracelet on your wrist, take the loop from the beginning of the bracelet and hook it over the knot and end bead at the other end.

38

The Natural Look

Alter the style of this simple bracelet dramatically by using natural-coloured suede cord and natural wood beads.

Moondance Ombré

Materials:

Designer: Claire Humpherson

90cm (36in) of blue and purple striped silk crepe ribbon

1 x titanium-plated button slider

1 x 12mm flat-back foiled crystal

Tools:

G-S Hypo cement

Instructions:

1 Tie a knot in the ribbon approximately 5–6cm (2–2¼in) from one end. Slide the button slider on to the ribbon until it sits next to the knot. Tie another knot on the other side of the slider to keep it in place.

2 Double over the other end of the ribbon and tie a knot to create a small loop.

3 Glue the crystal into the button slider. Leave to dry. To wear, wrap the ribbon around your wrist several times and hook the loop over the button.

Wild Raspberry Ombré

With vibrant colours and sparkling crystals, these bracelets are fun and easy to wear.

Boho Bangle

Materials:

Designer: Stacy Hunt

25 x 8mm purple dyed agate round beads

2 x silver-plated Zamak bangle bases

1 x silver-plated 'hope' charm

1 x Zamak irregular heart charm

1 x silver-plated charm carrier

1 x light purple suede tassel

1 x Zamak 8mm antique silver chaton
   charm setting

1 x purple 8mm purple
   crystal chaton

Purple organza ribbon

30cm (12in) of elastic stretch cord

3 x 7mm jump rings

Head pins

Tools:

Scissors

Clear nail varnish

G-S Hypo cement

Instructions:

1 Thread your agate round beads on to the elastic stretch cord to create a bracelet approximately the same size as one of the bangles. Add the charm carrier after your last bead.

2 Tie the ends of the elastic together to secure the bracelet. Add a dab of clear nail varnish for extra hold and cut off any excess elastic. Hide the knot inside the charm carrier.

3 Use jump rings and head pins to add your charms and tassel to the bangle and charm carrier. Tie your bangles and bracelet together with a piece of organza ribbon to finish.

Woodland Berry Bangle

Ring the changes by combining one silver bangle with two bracelets made from multi-coloured semi-precious beads, and link them with a pretty Liberty-print ribbon.

Wrap and Knot Bracelet

Materials:

Designer: Vicki Downes

2m (80in) of black 2mm round leather cord

6 x antique silver 6mm Zamak large-hole round beads

8 x large silver-plated fancy spacer beads

4 x silver-plated ball-end beads to fit 2mm cord

50cm (20in) of black 1mm waxed cotton cord

Tools:

Scissors

Clear contact glue

Instructions:

1 Cut five pieces of leather cord each 40cm (16in) long.

2 Gather the cords together and tie an overhand knot approximately 10cm (4in) from one end.

3 Thread on the beads in a random order, sometimes on to a single leather cord and sometimes on to pairs of cords.

4 Tie another overhand knot at the other end of the bracelet so that it is the right size for your wrist.

5 Cut off three of the five strand ends by each knot, leaving you with two strands on both sides.

6 Cross the two pairs of remaining strands and use the waxed cotton cord to make four square knots (see page 6) over them, forming a sliding knot.

7 Finish by trimming the ends and gluing on the four silver-plated ball-end beads.

Pearl and Gold Wrap
Use soft rose gold beads and pastel leather for a pretty feminine version of this bracelet.

Seashore Plait

Designer: Laura Bajor

Materials:

5m (200in) of blue double-sided suede cord

3 x seashore-themed antique silver charms,
e.g. starfish, turtle and seahorse

1 x antique silver Zamak daisy charm ring

3 x 6mm silver-plated jump rings

Tools:

Snipe nose pliers

Flat nose pliers

Scissors

G-S Hypo cement

Candy Floss Plait

*Change to pink suede and gold-plated
charms for a very different look.*

Instructions:

1 Cut the cord into two pieces of length 2.5m
(100in). Place them together and fold them
in half to create a loop. Tie the loop with an
overhand knot, making it large enough to pass
another knot through.

2 Use the four strands to create a four-strand
plait (braid) (see page 7).

3 Thread the daisy charm ring on to the end of
the bracelet and tie an overhand knot behind it
to secure.

4 Using your pliers, attach jump rings to the
charms. Attach the charms randomly to the
plaited (braided) bracelet.

5 Wrap the bracelet several times around your
wrist and pass the knot and the flower slider
through the loop to secure.

Author's note

We hope that you have enjoyed making some of the designs in this book – perhaps you have even been inspired to design a friendship bracelet of your own.

Although the components used in the designs are widely available, they can all be obtained from the Beads Direct website:
www.beadsdirect.co.uk
The specific components for each project are listed in the Design Centre on the website, under the name of each piece. If you need further help or details, please email Beads Direct Customer Service:
service@beadsdirect.co.uk

Beads Direct are a major online retailer of beads and jewellery-making accessories and supply worldwide.